The Bombing *of* Hiroshima

6 August 1945

The Bombing of Hiroshima

John Malam

CHERRYTREE
BOOKS

A Cherrytree Book

First published 2002
by Cherrytree Press
327 High Street
Slough
Berkshire
SLI ITX

First published in 2002

British Library Cataloguing in Publication Data
Malam, John.
  The Bombing of Hiroshima. - (Dates with history)
  1.Hiroshima-shi (Japan) - History - Bombardment, 1945-
    Juvenile literature
  I.Title
  940.5'4'25

ISBN 1842340999

To contact the author, send an email to:
johnmalam@aol.com
Editor: Louise John
Design: Neil Sayer

Picture credits:

Contents

The search for a super-bomb

The story of how the world's most terrible weapon was invented began many years before it was used in the Second World War in 1945. In 1896, the French scientist Henri Becquerel discovered that atoms – the tiny particles of solid matter from which everything is made – give off energy.

The world's scientists were fascinated by Becquerel's discovery, and they soon realised that atoms contained huge amounts of stored-up energy. In 1904 a British scientist, Frederick Soddy, wondered if energy from

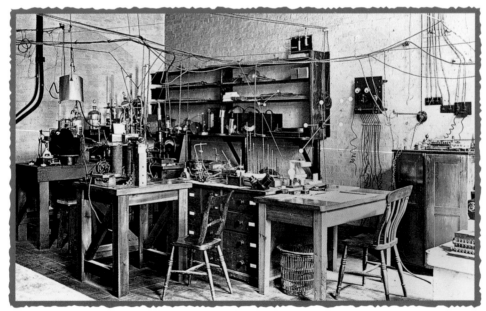

Much of the early work on splitting the atom would have been done in a science laboratory similar to this one.

atoms could be used to make a weapon. So, scientists in Europe and Scandinavia began the search to find a way to '**split the atom**'. Whoever succeeded would know how to force atoms to release their energy: they would have the secret for making an **atomic bomb**.

In August 1939, **Albert Einstein**, one of the world's cleverest scientists, wrote to the President of the United States of America, **Franklin D Roosevelt**. Einstein said:

World-famous scientist, Albert Einstein, talking about his ideas in 1935.

'*Sir… the element **uranium** may be turned into a new and important source of energy in the immediate future… This new phenomenon would also lead to the construction of bombs, and it is conceivable that extremely powerful bombs of a new type may thus be constructed.*'

One month after Einstein wrote to the President, the Second World War began. It ended six years later, in August 1945, when two bombs destroyed the Japanese cities of Hiroshima and Nagasaki. The bombs were atomic bombs, the deadliest weapon ever invented.

Splitting the atom

The 1930s were a time of great change in Germany because the Nazi Party, led by Adolf Hitler, had come to power. Under the Nazis, certain groups of people in Germany were persecuted, especially the Jewish community, many of whom sought refuge in the United States of America.

Amongst the Jews who fled from Nazi Germany were many scientists. They knew that German scientists were experimenting with a substance called uranium, and they

Nazi soldiers place notices on Jewish shops, urging German people not to buy Jewish goods.

feared that Germany was very close to building an atomic bomb.

In 1938, scientists in Germany did succeed in splitting the atom of uranium, a silvery-white metallic element. They worked out that if uranium atoms could be split over and over again, in a **chain reaction** over a very short period of time, the result would be a massive atomic explosion.

Leo Szilard reads a newspaper warning that the Russians might have made an atomic bomb.

On 1 September 1939, the German army invaded Poland. Two days later, on 3 September, Britain and France declared war on Germany and the Second World War began.

One month before the start of the war, three of the scientists who had fled to America, Leo Szilard, Eugene Wigner and Edward Teller, told Albert Einstein to write his letter to President Roosevelt. Einstein had also fled Nazi Germany and because he was world-famous the scientists hoped the President would be interested in what Einstein had to say. He was.

America enters the war

Even though the United States was at peace in 1939, President Roosevelt instructed his officials to look into Einstein's suggestions.

At first, the war was a war between the powers of Europe and there seemed no reason why the United States should become involved. However, on 19 October 1939, President Roosevelt replied to Einstein. He wanted the USA to be first to develop an atomic bomb, not Germany. The letter said:

*'My dear Professor,
I want to thank you for your recent letter… I found this data of such import that I have convened a Board… to thoroughly investigate the possibilities of your suggestion regarding the element of uranium.'*

The American effort to build an atomic bomb got off to a slow start, mainly because the USA was not involved in the war and there was no urgency to develop it. This changed on 7 December 1941 when, without warning,

Japanese war planes attacked US Navy ships at their Pearl Harbor base, on the Pacific island of Hawaii. Some 2,400 American servicemen and civilians were killed.

Japan was already fighting a war with China, and to keep its army supplied it had been buying scrap metal and oil from America. In 1940, Japan declared its support for Germany. So in July 1941, America stopped sending war supplies to Japan. This angered the Japanese government, who began to plan the raid on Pearl Harbor. When the attack came, it brought the USA into the Second World War.

US Navy ships are bombed during the attack on Pearl Harbor, Hawaii.

The Manhattan Project

At about the same time as the Pearl Harbor attack, a top-secret project began in the USA. It was code-named the Manhattan Project, after the district of Manhattan in the city of New York where it had its first headquarters. Its aim was simple: to build an atomic bomb before the enemy did.

Work on the Manhattan Project was soon under way between the Americans and the British. There was an added urgency to their work since both sides thought Germany was very close to building an atomic bomb. However, what no one in America or Britain knew at the time was that Germany had actually decided *not* to build an atomic bomb. German officials thought it would be too expensive – and they believed they would win the war, anyway.

In November 1942, the head of the Manhattan Project, **General Leslie R. Groves**, and the project's top scientist, **Dr Robert Oppenheimer**, chose a site for their main laboratory at Los Alamos, a small town in the mountains of New Mexico, USA. It was chosen because it was far away from large towns and cities, and

The high-security, top-secret laboratory at Los Alamos opened in April 1943.

there were desert areas where explosions could be
let off in secret.

Building an atomic bomb required money – the project
cost an estimated $2 billion. It also needed people. By
1944, around 129,000 people were working on the
Manhattan Project, but only a few knew what they
were building.

The Los Alamos laboratory produced two atomic bombs,
each of a different type. One used uranium to produce
an explosion and the other used **plutonium** – another
silvery-white, metallic element. The scientists gave
nicknames to the bombs. The uranium bomb was named
Little Boy, because of its long, thin shape. The plutonium
bomb, which was much rounder, was named Fat Man.

Models of the Little Boy (left) and Fat Man (right) atomic bombs.

Testing the atomic bomb

America's atomic bombs were finished by the end of 1944 – but would they work? In the south of New Mexico, 370km from Los Alamos, was the remote Alamogordo Bombing Range, where the US military tried out new weapons. It was here, in an area code-named Trinity, that the world's first atomic bomb was tested.

The Trinity Test took place at dawn on 16 July 1945, when a plutonium test-bomb, nicknamed Jumbo, was detonated at the top of a 30m-tall tower. It exploded with the force of 19,000 tonnes of ordinary explosives. A flash of light brighter than anything ever seen on Earth before lit up the desert, and 425 scientists and technicians watched as a huge fireball became a

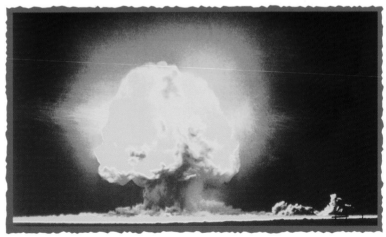

The mushroom-shaped cloud of the Trinity Test explosion rose 12,200m into the sky.

mushroom-shaped cloud. The temperature at Ground Zero – the place directly underneath the bomb tower – was three times as hot as the Sun, and a crater measuring 730m across was blasted into the New Mexico desert. America's atomic bomb worked. A deadly super-bomb had been created.

Only after the war did Robert Oppenheimer's part in the Manhattan Project become public knowledge. This is what he said about the Trinity Test explosion:

Robert Oppenheimer (right) and General Groves stand at the remains of the tower on which the first atomic bomb was detonated.

'We waited until the blast had passed, walked out of the shelter and then it was extremely solemn. We knew the world would not be the same. A few people laughed, a few people cried. Most people were silent. I remembered the line from the Hindu scripture, the Bhagavad-Gita: ... "Now I am become Death, the destroyer of worlds". I suppose we all thought that, one way or another.'

An important meeting

At the start of the Manhattan Project in 1942, Germany was the most likely future target for an atomic bomb. However, as the war progressed, America and Britain realised that Germany was not going to build an atomic bomb of its own. By early 1945, Germany was close to defeat. Hitler killed himself in April, and on 8 May, Germany surrendered. The war in Europe was over, but the Pacific war – the war between America and Japan – raged on.

On 17 July 1945, the day after the Trinity Test, a conference began at Potsdam, a town near Berlin, the German capital. At the meeting were the leaders of the countries that had defeated Germany: the new President of America, **Harry**

Devastation in the Japanese capital city of Tokyo caused by fire-bombs during the Pacific war.

From left to right, leaders Churchill, Truman and Stalin, photographed at the Potsdam Conference, 1945.

S Truman, the British Prime Minister, **Winston Churchill** and **Josef Stalin**, leader of the Soviet Union.

At the Potsdam Conference, the victorious leaders talked about the rebuilding of Europe. They were concerned with what to do about the defeated Germany and where to place borders for the countries involved in the war, particularly Poland. The main talking point, however, was how to end the Pacific war.

A secret plan

President Truman learned about the successful test-firing of the atomic bomb while he was at the Potsdam Conference. He was pleased the test had gone so well. To his way of thinking the atomic bomb could be used to bring the war in the Pacific to a quick end and, therefore, save American lives. However, he had to take into account a difficult political situation.

The problem was that the Soviet Union was not at war with Japan. However, at the Potsdam Conference, Josef

Harry S Truman became the 33rd President of the USA after President Roosevelt died in April 1945.

A US Marine aims his machine gun at a Japanese sniper during the battle of Okinawa in the Pacific war.

Stalin agreed to join forces with America and Britain and go to war against Japan. The Soviet Union would declare war on Japan by 15 August and the plan was for American, British, and Soviet forces to invade Japan. But there was another plan, which the Soviet Union knew nothing about.

President Truman had something else in mind. Now that America had the atomic bomb, perhaps he didn't need help from the Soviet Union after all. The fact is, America and the Soviet Union didn't really trust each other. Both wanted to become major world powers after the war, and now that America had the atomic bomb, President Truman knew he had something the Soviet Union didn't. This was the political reason why America wanted to use its new weapon – to get the 'upper hand' over the Soviet Union.

The target cities

The city of Hiroshima in 1930, before the atomic bomb was dropped.

On 21 July 1945, five days after the Trinity Test, and while President Truman was still at the Potsdam Conference, he gave the go-ahead for the atomic bomb to be used. It was to be used before 15 August, which was when the Soviet Union had said they would enter the war against Japan.

Before the Potsdam Conference ended, Japan was given a chance to surrender. Japan refused. The conference ended on 2 August and the events that took place over the following seven days were to change the course of history. While plans for the invasion of Japan were going ahead, secret preparations had already been made to use the atomic bomb.

American military leaders decided that the atomic bomb should be dropped in broad daylight, and only if the weather was good. Also, it should be used against a city that had not already been damaged by **conventional bombs**. This way the full force of an atomic explosion would be seen, and Japan would be so shocked it would surrender.

Four Japanese cities were chosen as targets. They were, in this order: Kyoto, Hiroshima, Kokura, and Niigata. Objections were raised about bombing Kyoto, an ancient city of great religious importance to the Japanese, so it was removed from the list. Kyoto was spared, and Hiroshima became first choice. The city of Nagasaki was added instead, in fourth place on the list. Instructions were issued to the US Air Force not to drop fire bombs on the target cities – they were to be left alone.

A map of Japan showing the target cities for the atomic bomb.

HOKKAIDO

N

Niigata

HONSHU Tokyo

J O   A   P   A   N

Kyoto

Hiroshima

Kokura

Nagasaki

SHIKOKU

KYUSHU

🌟 Atomic bomb explosion

● Potential bomb target

■ Capital city

0   200 miles

0   300 km

Hiroshima is bombed

On the afternoon of 5 August 1945, President Truman gave the order to drop the atomic bomb on the city of Hiroshima. Hours later, at 2.45am on 6 August, a B-29 bomber took off from an American airfield on the Pacific island of Tinian, 2,740km from its target. On board the plane, flown by Colonel Paul W Tibbets, was the Little Boy atomic bomb. Flying behind the bomber were two observation planes, carrying cameras and scientific instruments.

*Colonel Paul W Tibbets stands beside his plane, the **Enola Gay**, which was named after his mother.*

For some weeks before Hiroshima was bombed, an American weather plane had flown high over the city. The city's residents had got used to hearing the air-raid sirens sound at the same time each day and they had got used to seeing the lone plane circling above them. When the sirens sounded at 7.00am on the

Crewmen of the Enola Gay *load the Little Boy atomic bomb onto the plane, on the evening before it was dropped.*

morning of 6 August, the weather plane could be seen, as usual. There did not seem to be any cause for alarm.

The *Enola Gay* reached Hiroshima at 7.30am. The weather was good, and the American bomber circled in the bright, cloudless sky at a height of around 9,500m above the city.

At 8.15am, Little Boy was dropped on Hiroshima. The aiming point was the Aioi Bridge in the city centre. No warning had been given to the city's 350,000 inhabitants. To them, it was an ordinary Monday morning, the start of a new week. They could have had no idea what one 3m-long bomb was going to do to them and their city.

Death of a city and its people

As soon as the *Enola Gay* had released Little Boy, the plane turned steeply and flew from the scene. It took about a minute for Little Boy to fall by parachute to the point at which it exploded. It was not designed to hit the ground. Instead, it blew up at about 580m above Hiroshima. It had the same force as 12,500 tonnes of conventional explosives.

Inside the *Enola Gay*, bright light from the explosion filled the plane. Colonel Tibbets and his crew turned to look back at Hiroshima. They wore Polaroid goggles to protect their eyes from the blinding flash of light. Tibbets said: *'The city was hidden by that awful cloud... boiling up, mushrooming.'* Captain Robert Lewis, the co-pilot, said: *'My God, what have we done?'*

The mushroom cloud from the atomic explosion rising into the sky above the city of Hiroshima.

No one knows exactly how many people died as a result of the atomic explosion at Hiroshima on 6 August 1945. Most estimates say that 70,000 people died instantly – from the heat and the blast. The explosion caused a wind that blew at 440 metres per second and the temperature reached 5,000°C.

More deadly still was the effect of radiation – an invisible force released by the bomb that entered people's bodies and caused them to die days, weeks, months, and years after the bombing. In 1946, a report put the civilian death toll at 118,661. Some estimates say the present death toll is as high as 200,000.

As for Hiroshima itself, 90 per cent of the city's buildings were destroyed.

A bleak view of the city of Hiroshima after the bombing.

Nagasaki is bombed

Three days after the bombing of Hiroshima, Nagasaki suffered the same fate. A B-29 bomber, nicknamed *Bockscar,* piloted by Major Charles W Sweeney, set off for the city of Kokura, carrying the Fat Man atomic bomb. But Kokura was hidden by cloud, so the plane was diverted to Nagasaki.

Fat Man fell by parachute towards the unsuspecting city. At 11.02 on the morning of 9 August 1945, it exploded

Japanese delegates sign the official documents of surrender.

500m above the ground. It had the same force as 22,000 tonnes of ordinary explosives. About 270,000 people lived in Nagasaki and an estimated 75,000 died. In the years that followed, the death toll increased to 150,000. One third of the city was destroyed.

The day before the bombing, the Soviet Union declared war on Japan. Faced with this, and with America using its super-bomb, Japan surrendered on 14 August. The Second World War was over and the atomic bomb had changed the world for ever.

Postscript

Was it necessary to use the atomic bomb? Even after all this time, opinions are divided between those for it and those against it.

President Truman, the politician who gave the order to drop the bomb said: *'This is the greatest thing in history.'* Leo Szilard, the scientist who worked on the bomb, said: *'Using atomic bombs against Japan is one of the greatest blunders of history.'* Albert Einstein, whose letter encouraged America to build the bomb, said: *'I could burn my fingers that I wrote that first letter to Roosevelt.'*

Sankichi Toge wrote this famous poem. He died in 1953, from leukemia caused by radiation. He was a victim of the Hiroshima bomb.

Give Back the Human
Give back my father, give back my mother;
Give back my elders;
Give me my sons and daughters back.
Give me back myself,
Give back the human race.
As long as this life lasts, this life,
Give back peace
That will never end.

Timeline

1938   Otto Hahn and Fritz Strassmann of Germany split the uranium atom.

1939   *2 August:* Albert Einstein writes to President Roosevelt with news about the potential for building a bomb with uranium.

1939   *3 September:* The Second World War begins.

1939   *19 October:* President Roosevelt replies to Einstein.

1941   *9 October:* President Roosevelt decides that America should build an atomic bomb.

1941   *6 December:* The Manhattan Project begins, with the aim of building America's atomic bomb.

1941   *7 December:* America enters the war after Japan attacks the US naval base at Pearl Harbor, Hawaii.

1942   *16 November:* Los Alamos, New Mexico, USA, is chosen as the place for the atomic bomb laboratory.

1945   *12 April:* President Roosevelt dies. Harry S Truman becomes the new President of the USA.

1945   *8 May:* Germany surrenders. War in Europe ends.

1945   *16 July:* First atomic device is successfully tested, at Alamogordo, New Mexico (Trinity Test).

1945   *17 July:* The Potsdam Conference begins.

1945   *21 July:* President Truman approves an order for atomic bombs to be used.

1945	*25 July:* US Air Force is given written instructions for the bombing of cities in Japan.
1945	*26 July:* Japan is told to surrender.
1945	*28 July:* Japan refuses to surrender.
1945	*2 August:* The Potsdam Conference ends.
1945	*6 August:* An atomic bomb is dropped on Hiroshima.
1945	*8 August:* The Soviet Union declares war on Japan.
1945	*9 August:* An atomic bomb is dropped on Nagasaki.
1945	*14 August:* Japan surrenders. The Second World War ends.
1945	*2 September:* Japan signs the surrender documents.

The A-Bomb Dome, Hiroshima, as it is today. The atomic bomb exploded above it.

Glossary

atomic bomb An explosive device in which a great amount of energy is released in a very short space of time.

chain reaction A process in which one reaction causes another reaction to occur, which, in turn, produces a further reaction, and so on. The reactions are all linked together.

conventional bomb A device that uses 'ordinary' explosives, of which there are many types.

plutonium A silvery-white metallic substance used in the making of the atomic bomb. It is man-made and does not occur in nature.

split the atom A process in which atoms are made to release energy in a chain reaction, leading to an atomic explosion.

uranium A silvery-white metallic substance found in nature which was used in the making of the atomic bomb.

Who's Who?

Sir Winston Churchill
British Prime Minister from 1940 to 1945, and from 1951 to 1955.

Albert Einstein
German-born, Nobel Prize-winning Jewish scientist. In the 1930s he fled to the USA, becoming a US citizen in 1940.

General Leslie R Groves
American head of the Manhattan Project from 1942 until 1947.

Dr Robert Oppenheimer
American physicist and director of the Los Alamos laboratory.

Franklin D Roosevelt
The 32nd President of the USA. Under him America began to build the atomic bomb.

Josef Stalin
Head of state of the Soviet Union, during the Second World War.

Harry S Truman
The 33rd President of the USA. He gave the order to use the atomic bomb against Japan.

Index

6 August 1945 6 August 1945 6 August 1945 6 August 1945 6 August 1945 6 August 1945 6 August
945 6 August 1945 6 August 1945 6 August 1945 6 August 1945 6 August 1945 6 August 1945 6 Aug
st 1945 6 August 1945 6 August 1945 6 August 1945 6 August 1945 6 August 1945 6 August 1945 6
ugust 1945 6 August 1945 6 August 1945 6 August 1945 6 August 1945 6 August 1945 6 August 194
6 August 1945 6 August 1945 6 August 1945 6 August 1945 6 August 1945 6 August 1945 6 August
945 6 August 1945 6 August 1945 6 August 1945 6 August 1945 6 August 1945 6 August 1945 6 Aug
st 1945 6 August 1945 6 August 1945 6 August 1945 6 August 1945 6 August 1945 6 August 1945 6
ugust 1945 6 August 1945 6 August 1945 6 August 1945 6 August 1945 6 August 1945 6 August 194
6 August 1945 6 August 1945 6 August 1945 6 August 1945 6 August 1945 6 August 1945 6 August
945 6 August 1945 6 August 1945 6 August 1945 6 August 1945 6 August 1945 6 August 1945 6 Aug
st 1945 6 August 1945 6 August 1945 6 August 1945 6 August 1945 6 August 1945 6 August 1945 6
ugust 1945 6 August 1945 6 August 1945 6 August 1945 6 August 1945 6 August 1945 6 August 194
6 August 1945 6 August 1945 6 August 1945 6 August 1945 6 August 1945 6 August 1945 6 August
945 6 August 1945 6 August 1945 6 August 1945 6 August 1945 6 August 1945 6 August 1945 6 Aug
st 1945 6 August 1945 6 August 1945 6 August 1945 6 August 1945 6 August 1945 6 August 1945 6
ugust 1945 6 August 1945 6 August 1945 6 August 1945 6 August 1945 6 August 1945 6 August 194
6 August 1945 6 August 1945 6 August 1945 6 August 1945 6 August 1945 6 August 1945 6 August
945 6 August 1945 6 August 1945 6 August 1945 6 August 1945 6 August 1945 6 August 1945 6 Aug
st 1945 6 August 1945 6 August 1945 6 August 1945 6 August 1945 6 August 1945 6 August 1945 6
ugust 1945 6 August 1945 6 August 1945 6 August 1945 6 August 1945 6 August 1945 6 August 194
6 August 1945 6 August 1945 6 August 1945 6 August 1945 6 August 1945 6 August 1945 6 August
945 6 August 1945 6 August 1945 6 August 1945 6 August 1945 6 August 1945 6 August 1945 6 Aug
st 1945 6 August 1945 6 August 1945 6 August 1945 6 August 1945 6 August 1945 6 August 1945 6
ugust 1945 6 August 1945 6 August 1945 6 August 1945 6 August 1945 6 August 1945 6 August 194
6 August 1945 6 August 1945 6 August 1945 6 August 1945 6 August 1945 6 August 1945 6 August
945 6 August 1945 6 August 1945 6 August 1945 6 August 1945 6 August 1945 6 August 1945 6 Aug
st 1945 6 August 1945 6 August 1945 6 August 1945 6 August 1945 6 August 1945 6 August 1945 6
ugust 1945 6 August 1945 6 August 1945 6 August 1945 6 August 1945 6 August 1945 6 August 194
6 August 1945 6 August 1945 6 August 1945 6 August 1945 6 August 1945 6 August 1945 6 August
945 6 August 1945 6 August 1945 6 August 1945 6 August 1945 6 August 1945 6 August 1945 6 Aug
st 1945 6 August 1945 6 August 1945 6 August 1945 6 August 1945 6 August 1945 6 August 1945 6
ugust 1945 6 August 1945 6 August 1945 6 August 1945 6 August 1945 6 August 1945 6 August 194
6 August 1945 6 August 1945 6 August 1945 6 August 1945 6 August 1945 6 August 1945 6 August
945 6 August 1945 6 August 1945 6 August 1945 6 August 1945 6 August 1945 6 August 1945 6 Aug
st 1945 6 August 1945 6 August 1945 6 August 1945 6 August 1945 6 August 1945 6 August 1945 6
ugust 1945 6 August 1945 6 August 1945 6 August 1945 6 August 1945 6 August 1945 6 August 194
6 August 1945 6 August 1945 6 August 1945 6 August 1945 6 August 1945 6 August 1945 6 August
945 6 August 1945 6 August 1945 6 August 1945 6 August 1945 6 August 1945 6 August 1945 6 Aug
st 1945 6 August 1945 6 August 1945 6 August 1945 6 August 1945 6 August 1945 6 August 1945 6
ugust 1945 6 August 1945 6 August 1945 6 August 1945 6 August 1945 6 August 1945 6 August 194
6 August 1945 6 August 1945 6 August 1945 6 August 1945 6 August 1945 6 August 1945 6 August
945 6 August 1945 6 August 1945 6 August 1945 6 August 1945 6 August 1945 6 August 1945 6 Aug
st 1945 6 August 1945 6 August 1945 6 August 1945 6 August 1945 6 August 1945 6 August 1945 6
ugust 1945 6 August 1945 6 August 1945 6 August 1945 6 August 1945 6 August 1945 6 August 194
6 August 1945 6 August 1945 6 August 1945 6 August 1945 6 August 1945 6 August 1945 6 August
945 6 August 1945 6 August 1945 6 August 1945 6 August 1945 6 August 1945 6 August 1945 6 Aug
st 1945 6 August 1945 6 August 1945 6 August 1945 6 August 1945 6 August 1945 6 August 1945 6
ugust 1945 6 August 1945 6 August 1945 6 August 1945 6 August 1945 6 August 1945 6 August 194
6 August 1945 6 August 1945 6 August 1945 6 August 1945 6 August 1945 6 August 1945 6 August
945 6 August 1945 6 August 1945 6 August 1945 6 August 1945 6 August 1945 6 August 1945 6 Aug
st 1945 6 August 1945 6 August 1945 6 August 1945 6 August 1945 6 August 1945 6 August 1945 6
ugust 1945 6 August 1945 6 August 1945 6 August 1945 6 August 1945 6 August 1945 6 August 194
6 August 1945 6 August 1945 6 August 1945 6 August 1945 6 August 1945 6 August 1945 6 August
945 6 August 1945 6 August 1945 6 August 1945 6 August 1945 6 August 1945 6 August 1945 6 Aug
st 1945 6 August 1945 6 August 1945 6 August 1945 6 August 1945 6 August 1945 6 August 1945 6
ugust 1945 6 August 1945 6 August 1945 6 August 1945 6 August 1945 6 August 1945 6 August 194
6 August 1945 6 August 1945 6 August 1945 6 August 1945 6 August 1945 6 August 1945 6 August
945 6 August 1945 6 August 1945 6 August 1945 6 August 1945 6 August 1945 6 August 1945 6 Aug
st 1945 6 August 1945 6 August 1945 6 August 1945 6 August 1945 6 August 1945 6 August 1945 6
ugust 1945 6 August 1945 6 August 1945 6 August 1945 6 August 1945 6 August 1945 6 August 194
6 August 1945 6 August 1945 6 August 1945 6 August 1945 6 August 1945 6 August 1945 6 August
945 6 August 1945 6 August 1945 6 August 1945 6 August 1945 6 August 1945 6 August 1945 6 Aug
st 1945 6 August 1945 6 August 1945 6 August 1945 6 August 1945 6 August 1945 6 August 1945 6
August 1945 6 August 1945 6 August 1945 6 August 1945 6 August 1945 6 August 1945 6 August 194
6 August 1945 6 August 1945 6 August 1945 6 August 1945 6 August 1945 6 August 1945 6 August
945 6 August 1945 6 August 1945 6 August 1945 6 August 1945 6 August 1945 6 August 1945 6 Aug
st 1945 6 August 1945 6 August 1945 6 August 1945 6 August 1945 6 August 1945 6 August 1945 6
August 1945 6 August 1945 6 August 1945 6 August 1945 6 August 1945 6 August 1945 6 August 194
6 August 1945 6 August 1945 6 August 1945 6 August 1945 6 August 1945 6 August 1945 6 August
945 6 August 1945 6 August 1945 6 August 1945 6 August 1945 6 August 1945 6 August 1945 6 Aug
st 1945 6 August 1945 6 August 1945 6 August 1945 6 August 1945 6 August 1945 6 August 1945 6
August 1945 6 August 1945 6 August 1945 6 August 1945 6 August 1945 6 August 1945 6 August 194
5 6 August 1945 6 August 1945 6 August 1945 6 August 1945 6 August 1945 6 August 1945 6 August
945 6 August 1945 6 August 1945 6 August 1945 6 August 1945 6 August 1945 6 August 1945 6 Aug
st 1945 6 August 1945 6 August 1945 6 August 1945 6 August 1945 6 August 1945 6 August 1945 6
August 1945 6 August 1945 6 August 1945 6 August 1945 6 August 1945 6 August 1945 6 August 194
945 6 August 1945 6 August 1945 6 August 1945 6 August 1945 6 August 1945 6 August 1945 6 Aug